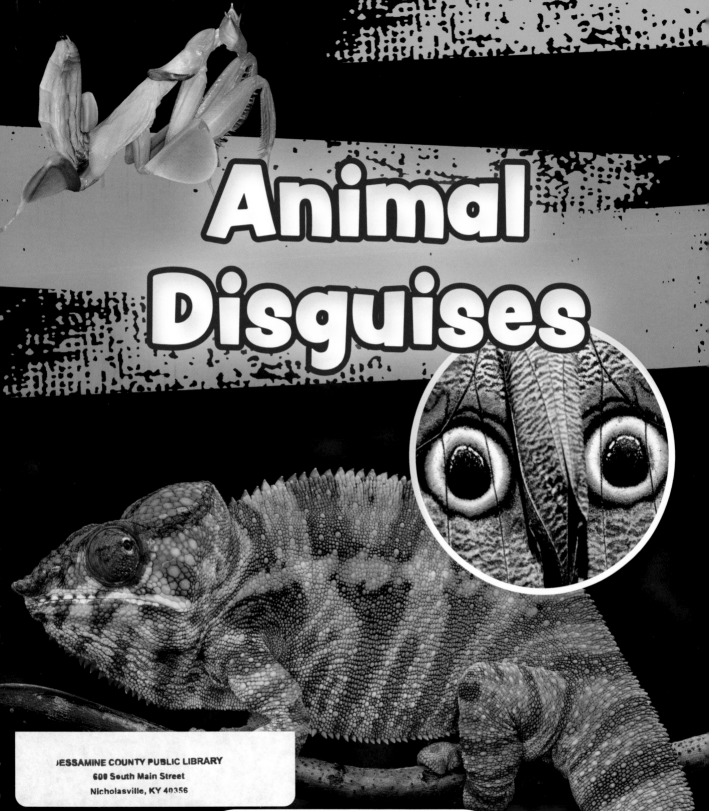

Animal Disguises

Natalie Hyde

Crabtree Publishing Company

www.crabtreebooks.com

CRABTREE
PUBLISHING COMPANY
WWW.CRABTREEBOOKS.COM

Author:
Natalie Hyde
Editorial director:
Kathy Middleton
Editor:
Sonya Newland
Proofreaders:
Izzi Howell, Crystal Sikkens
Graphic design:
Clare Nicholas
Image research:
Natalie Hyde and Sonya Newland
Production coordinator and prepress:
Tammy McGarr
Print coordinator:
Katherine Berti

Images:
Alamy: 10 (Dennis Cox), 11b (Anett Flassig), 12 (Avalon/Photoshot License). 17l (Arco Images GmbH), 21b (John Porter LRPS), 23b (Paul Wood); Getty Images: 24–25, 25t (George Grall), 25b (Ed Reschke); Shutterstock: 4l (Katarina Christenson), 4r (Kawin Jiaranaisakul), 5tl (irin-k), 5tr (Allocricetulus), 5b (Ang Kean Leng), 6 (Vince Adam), 7t (Art65395), 7b (Niney Azman), 8 (Jacqueline Lee), 9l (Michael Warwick), 9r (ymgerman), 11t (Edwin Butter), 13tl (Andrew Astbury), 13tr (Sophia Granchinho), 13b (Jiri Hrebicek), 14 (Arto Hakola), 14–15 (Ondrej Prosicky), 15t (Jan Bures), 15b (Nasaza), 16 (ideation90), 17r (Brian Lasenby), 18 (Dario Sabljak), 19tl (kaschibo), 19tr (Bildagentur Zoonar GmbH), 19b (Luke Suen), 20 (Alta Oosthuizen), 20–21 background (205825768), 20–21 (Michael Potter11), 21t (Daniel Zuppinger), 22 (Jay Ondreicka), 23t (Dennis W Donohue), 26 (Connie Kouwenhoven), 27t (Vladimir Wrangel), 27b (PRILL), 28 (Christopher MacDonald), 29t (Action Sports Photography), 29b (Lori Ellis).

Library and Archives Canada Cataloguing in Publication

Title: Animal disguises / Natalie Hyde.
Names: Hyde, Natalie, 1963- author.
Description: Series statement: Astonishing animals |
  Includes bibliographical references and index.
Identifiers: Canadiana (print) 20200155105 | Canadiana (ebook) 20200155113 |
  ISBN 9780778769170 (hardcover) |
  ISBN 9780778769354 (softcover) |
  ISBN 9781427124357 (HTML)
Subjects: LCSH: Animal defenses—Juvenile literature. | LCSH: Camouflage
  (Biology)—Juvenile literature. | LCSH: Mimicry (Biology)—Juvenile literature. |
  LCSH: Animals—Adaptation—Juvenile literature.
Classification: LCC QL759 .H93 2020 | DDC j591.47—dc23

Library of Congress Cataloging-in-Publication Data

Names: Hyde, Natalie, 1963- author.
Title: Animal disguises / Natalie Hyde.
Description: New York, New York : Crabtree Publishing Company, [2020] |
  Series: Astonishing animals | Includes index.
Identifiers: LCCN 2019053189 (print) | LCCN 2019053190 (ebook) |
  ISBN 9780778769170 (hardcover) |
  ISBN 9780778769354 (paperback) |
  ISBN 9781427124357 (ebook)
Subjects: LCSH: Camouflage (Biology)--Juvenile literature. |
  Mimicry (Biology)--Juvenile literature. |
  Animals--Adaptation--Juvenile literature.
Classification: LCC QL767 .H93 2020 (print) | LCC QL767 (ebook) |
  DDC 591.47/2--dc23
LC record available at https://lccn.loc.gov/2019053189
LC ebook record available at https://lccn.loc.gov/2019053190

Crabtree Publishing Company

www.crabtreebooks.com   1-800-387-7650

Printed in the U.S.A./022020/CG20200102

Published in Canada
Crabtree Publishing
616 Welland Ave.
St. Catharines, Ontario
L2M 5V6

Published in the United States
Crabtree Publishing
PMB 59051
350 Fifth Avenue, 59th Floor
New York, New York 10118

Published in the United Kingdom
Crabtree Publishing
Maritime House
Basin Road North, Hove
BN41 1WR

Published in Australia
Crabtree Publishing
Unit 3 – 5 Currumbin Court
Capalaba
QLD 4157

Table of contents

Amazing disguises

It's amazing to see unusual animals living in the wild. It's also amazing to *not* see animals in the wild! That's because some creatures have incredible ways of disguising themselves like their environment, or even like other animals!

Search and find

Some animals use **cunning camouflage** to blend into the background in their environment. Take a look at this picture. Can you see the moth on the bark? These clever creatures move around on the tree until they find the spot where they will be the least visible!

Even experts don't know how moths find just the right spot to hide in plain sight.

The common baron caterpillar is almost invisible to the birds that like to eat them. Are your eyes better than those birds? Can you spot the caterpillar?

Eat or be eaten

Many types of moths disguise themselves to hide from **predators**. But there are other reasons for putting on a disguise. Some animals use their coloring to trick their predators into staying away by looking bigger, more powerful, or not tasty to eat. Some clever creatures can even disguise the sounds they make, to mimic animals that a predator would not want to eat!

Spot the difference! Harmless hoverflies (bottom) have the same color and pattern as wasps (top). Their coloring fools predators into thinking they taste bad and can sting.

Ant-mimicking spiders have a similar body shape to an ant, and they pretend their two front legs are antennae!

Disguised as a harmless ant, these spiders can get within biting distance of their **prey**.

Orchid mantises

What beautiful pink-and-white flower is actually a **ferocious** predator? The orchid mantis! Disguised as a blossom, this insect preys on unsuspecting animals walking or flying by.

Orchid mantises can fly, but they prefer to sit and wait for their meals to come to them.

Beautiful danger

The orchid mantis is so well camouflaged that it wasn't discovered until 1879! A British explorer was studying flowers in Indonesia when he saw what looked like a flower eating a butterfly. Peering closer, he realized that it was actually an insect that looked exactly like an orchid!

These amazing insects blend in with orchids and other flowers.

Orchid mantises have been nicknamed "walking flower mantises."

Swaying in the breeze

Orchid mantises are usually yellow, white, orange, or light purple to match the flowers they pretend to be. These insects search for hunting spots on leaves and flowers. When one finds a spot, it grabs on with its back pair of legs and sways slightly to imitate flowers in the breeze. Then it waits for its meal to come right to it!

Orchid mantises snatch their insect prey out of the air with their front legs and devour it immediately.

While they mostly eat small insects, some orchid mantises catch and eat larger creatures such as frogs, lizards, and birds!

Wow!

Orchid mantises have tiny teeth that they use to rip their much bigger prey, such as frogs or mice, into small pieces.

Leafy seadragons

Stunning seaweed disguise

What's the best way to conceal yourself in the ocean if there is nowhere to hide? Disguise yourself as seaweed!

Keeping safe

Leafy seadragons do not use their frills to move—they have two other fins for swimming. But these small, almost invisible fins don't help them swim swiftly. So their camouflage is important to keep them safe from predators, such as large fish. These interesting sea horses can even change their color to blend in with their habitat, but they can't do this so well when they get old or sick.

Papa knows best

Like other types of sea horse, male leafy seadragons look after the eggs. They hold the eggs under their tails. Once the eggs hatch, the young are on their own. Leafy seadragons are on the **endangered** species list. They are often caught accidentally in fishing nets, and are also collected to be kept as pets.

Other animals that use camouflage hide by staying still, but the leafy seadragon hides by moving like floating seaweed.

A leafy seadragon's fins are so thin that they are practically see-through.

snout

FACT FILE

Found in: Southern and western coasts of Australia

Habitat: Near kelp-covered rocks and clumps of sea grass

Length: 8–9.5 inches (20–24 cm)

Diet: Small **crustaceans** such as tiny shrimp and plankton

frills

Leafy seadragons may use little bony spines along their backs to protect themselves.

Unlike other sea horses, leafy seadragons cannot curl their tails to hang on to objects.

Wow!

Seadragons do not have teeth or a stomach! They suck up their food with their pipe-like **snout**.

Owl butterflies

Are you being watched? In fact, those eyes aren't eyes at all! They're eye spots on the wings of a butterfly, who uses them as an **ingenious** disguise!

Amazing eye spots to confuse predators

The owl butterfly is active at sunrise and sunset, when its bird predators do not usually hunt.

Their brown color helps them blend into the bark of trees, where they rest.

I've got my eye on you!

Owl butterflies can only fly a few feet at a time. This makes them easy prey for birds. To protect themselves, they have two large eye spots on their wings. When they sit to feed, they look like large owls. This makes birds think twice about trying to attack them!

Owl, snake, or lizard?

Owl butterflies have patterns and colors that allow them to look like other creatures, too. The pattern on the corners of their wings resembles snakeskin, while smaller eyespots on the wings resemble the eyes of a lizard. Why imitate one animal when you can supersize your safety by imitating three?!

Wow!

The butterfly's large size makes its wide-eyed camouflage more convincing. These insects can have a wingspan of nearly 8 inches (20 cm)!

By flapping its wings and flashing its "eyes," the butterfly startles predators and gains valuable seconds to escape.

Predators usually attack the head—a vulnerable place. Having "eyes" on their wings makes a predator attack there, giving the butterfly a better chance of survival.

What do you see: a butterfly, or the head of a snake, lizard, or owl?

Arctic foxes

Is that a moving snow mound? No—it's a perfectly camouflaged Arctic fox! The animal's white winter coat makes it almost impossible to see in the frozen landscape.

Winter wardrobe

In the summer, when the Arctic **tundra** is covered in rocks and plants, the fur of the Arctic fox is light brown or gray. But come winter, it turns white to match its snowy habitat. The fur keeps the fox warm in temperatures as low as −94°F (−70°C)! That's super important for an animal that doesn't **hibernate** during winter.

The Arctic fox is also known as the polar fox, white fox, or snow fox.

The Arctic fox is the smallest wild member of the **canid** family in North America. Canids include wolves, foxes, and dogs.

In the worst storms, they can tunnel under the snow to keep out of the icy wind.

I'm so blue!

Some Arctic foxes have a dark, bluish-gray coat in summer and a pale, bluish-gray coat in winter. Foxes with this coloring are mostly found near Arctic waters. The bluish color helps them blend in with their **marine** environment.

Arctic foxes stay silent most of the time, but they can communicate with a barking yowl that can be heard far away.

The Arctic fox is the only canid to have fur on its foot pads to help it stay warm.

Arctic foxes' summer camouflage is as effective as their winter one, helping them blend in with the rocks!

Wow!

The Arctic fox raises its pups in networks of dens that are so huge they may have around 100 entrances!

13

Chameleons

Why waste time running after prey when you can blend into the background and silently wait for dinner to come to you? Chameleons have perfected the technique of flicking out their extra-long tongue to catch their food while remaining perfectly still.

Chameleons have two layers in their skin. The top layer contains a network of crystals. As the crystals move, different amounts of light are reflected off them, changing the color of the chameleon's skin.

Color match

It's a **myth** that chameleons can change their color to match their background. They couldn't camouflage themselves to look like a tablecloth or a checkerboard, for example! But they do have an amazing number of color combinations they can use as a disguise, including pink, blue, red, orange, yellow, and green. They pick the color mix that blends best with their environment.

A resting chameleon usually looks green.

Secret language

Chameleons do not just change color to hide. They use different colors to express their feelings, to heat up and cool down, or to communicate. For example, chameleons can change color to show they are angry or frightened. Males use bright colors to attract a female. Females can use color to show they are interested in a male, or to indicate they are pregnant!

FACT FILE

Found in: Africa and Madagascar

Habitat: Rain forests, savannas, and deserts

Length: 0.59–27 inches (1.5–69 cm)

Diet: Smaller types eat insects, larger ones eat lizards and birds

Some species of chameleon have tongues that are longer than their bodies!

A chameleon has five toes on each limb. Three toes group together on one side and two on the other, so the chameleon can grab onto branches easily.

Wow!

A chameleon's eyes move independently of each other, which allows it to scan its surroundings without moving its head.

15

Walking stick insects

Have you ever seen a twig get up and walk? If you did, it was most likely a walking stick insect!

Looks like a stick...feels like a stick...

Wooden acting

Walking stick insects take camouflage to a whole new level. They not only have the shape and color of twigs, but the texture of their body is also like wood! To help with their disguise, walking stick insects rock back and forth like real twigs on trees, swaying in the breeze.

Walking stick insects are a popular snack for spiders, lizards, birds, rodents, and even monkeys.

Some walking stick insect species play dead for hours to escape being eaten by predators.

16

Walking stick insects grow by **molting**, which means they shed their outer skin as they get bigger. They molt between four and eight times to reach maturity.

FACT FILE

Found: Worldwide, except Antarctica

Habitat: Tree canopies

Length: 0.6–22 inches (1.5–56 cm)

Diet: Leaves of trees and shrubs

Girl power!

Female stick insects can reproduce with a male or without one! If there is no male around, females can produce eggs on their own. These only grow into female young. In one species, scientists have never found any males! Sometimes ants will take the eggs to their nests and feed on them. But the ants only eat the outside of the eggs, and the baby inside is protected from other predators.

Wow!

If an attacker grabs a leg, the stick insect can shed it to get away! They grow a new leg when they molt. They cannot replace their limbs after they reach adulthood and stop molting.

The walking stick insect eats the skin it sheds during molting, in case a predator spots it and realizes the insect is close by!

Octopuses

Awesome color- and pattern- matching ability

Did that rock on the bottom of the sea just move? No, it was just an octopus camouflaged to look like a rock. The octopus is a master of disguise!

Blending in

Unlike many other clever camouflaging animals, octopuses can do more than just change their color. They can also alter the texture of their skin. They can create bumps, spikes, and ridges if these will help their disguise! Octopuses use their skill to either escape from predators or to sneak up on their prey.

Octopuses are sometimes called "chameleons of the sea."

If its environment is rocky and sharp, an octopus can make its skin look spiky to match.

Octopuses are good swimmers, but it is less exhausting for them to walk along the sea floor.

FACT FILE

Found in: Oceans worldwide

Habitat: Many including coral reefs, rocky areas, and sandy seabeds

Length: 1 inch–16 feet (2.5 cm–5 m)

Diet: Clams, shrimp, lobsters, fish, sharks, and even birds

A terrible fate awaits any creature that ignores the blue-ringed octopus's warning to stay away. It can release a poison that is deadly—even to humans.

Wow!

Octopuses can have two different colors and patterns at the same time. That means they can attract a mate with red on one side, while warning off a **rival** with white on the other!

Many reasons

Octopuses use color for all sorts of reasons. They change color to communicate or to attract a mate. The blue-ringed octopus (see above) makes bright blue rings appear on its skin as a warning to predators. The mimic octopus (see right) doesn't try to blend in to the background to hide. Instead, it changes to look like other creatures, including flounders, lionfish, and sea snakes.

The mimic octopus can disguise itself to look like more than 10 sea creatures, including a starfish!

Fork-tailed drongos

What's the laziest hunter in the bird world? The fork-tailed drongo! This trickster uses a devious disguise to save it the effort of hunting for itself!

Take-out meals

The drongo's disguise isn't its appearance, but its voice. It uses a vocal trick to fool animals such as meerkats into giving it a free meal. First, the drongo earns the meerkats' trust by giving a warning cry when it really spots a meerkat predator. The meerkats run and hide. But the next time the drongo gives the warning, it's a fake. The drongo waits until the meerkats have found lots of juicy insects, then sounds the alarm again. When the meerkats run away, the drongo steals their lunch!

If its targets start ignoring its false alarms, a drongo will often switch to the call of a panicked animal, which fools them again.

Fork-tailed drongos follow bush fires to eat the insects flying up to escape the flames. For this reason, they are sometimes called "fire birds."

20

The next level

The meerkats will only fall for this trick once, so the drongo has to change tactic. There is always one meerkat on guard duty. Next time, the drongo uses a different warning cry – a perfect imitation of the meerkat guard's own alarm call! The meerkats run for cover again, and the drongo helps itself to another meal of fresh scorpion or small snake!

FACT FILE

Found in: Africa, south of the Sahara Desert

Habitat: Open forest and bush

Length: 10 inches (25 cm)

Diet: Fish, insects, and large game leftovers

Drongos follow large animals like rhinos to feast on the insects they churn up as they move through the grass.

Wow!

Fork-tailed drongos have learned to mimic the calls of the young boys who herd cattle. This keeps the cattle moving, turning up lots of insects as they go!

Drongos do not like predators, such as leopards, in their area. They will follow them looking for a chance to sound the alarm and scare the big cat's prey.

Copperheads

When is a pile of dead leaves *not* a pile of dead leaves? When it's a copperhead snake curled up on the forest floor!

Like other poisonous snakes, copperheads are born with fangs and venom, ready to defend themselves!

A copperhead's light brown skin with reddish-brown patches makes it tricky to spot on the forest floor.

Pattern perfection

Thanks to the leaf-shaped patches on its body, when a copperhead is motionless among dead leaves or on clay earth, it is almost impossible to see! These snakes use their cunning camouflage to hide while they wait for prey to come their way.

Hide or bite?

Copperheads will bite when provoked. They are **venomous**, but their venom, or poison, is quite mild. It wouldn't kill a human, but it will stun or kill a small animal. In fact, copperheads more often "freeze" than bite. Most bites happen when someone steps on them accidentally because they can't see them. Maybe their camouflage is too good!

A copperhead's favorite feast is mice and voles, but they will also munch on lizards, small birds, insects, and even other snakes.

A copperhead often holds the prey in its mouth until it dies, then swallows it whole.

Wow!

Copperhead venom has been shown to stop cancer cells growing in tumors in mice. It has not yet been tested in humans.

Thorn bugs

Clever thorn bugs have found a good way to keep predators off their backs...by making it look like taking a bite out of them would be a painful experience!

Too painful to be prey

Thorn bugs also use their color as camouflage. They look bright and colorful up close, but from far away they look green and brown.

Safety in numbers

Thorn bugs are spiky little creatures, and their appearance puts off predators. After all, who wants to nibble on a thorn? These insects often group together on a branch. This makes the "thorny branch" look like a dangerous place to land for birds passing overhead—stopping them from swooping down to snack on the bugs!

Eat where you live

Thorn bugs don't have to go far to find food. Their beak-shaped mouths let them **pierce** the bark of the trees they sit on, to feed on the liquid called sap inside. After laying eggs under the bark, the female spends the rest of her six-week life guarding the eggs, and then the young, until they can defend themselves.

FACT FILE

Found in: Worldwide, but mostly in Florida, Mexico, northern South America

Habitat: Fruit trees

Length: 0.39 inches (1 cm)

Diet: Sap inside the trees they live on

A mother thornbug uses her club-shaped hind legs to kick at attackers.

Young thorn bugs have a chemical in their bodies that makes them taste bad to put off predators. The taste goes away when they become adults.

Baby thorn bugs have three horns, while adults only have one.

Wow!

Thorn bugs call to each other by sending vibrations along the stalks of the plant they are on. Mother thorn bugs use vibrations to warn their young of danger.

Stonefish

Watch out when you're wandering along the beach or paddling in the sea—those rocks around you may not be what they seem. Some might actually prove life-threatening!

Deadly venom

The venomous stonefish is covered in rough-looking brown or gray skin with red, orange, or yellow patches. These fish look so much like rocks that predators, prey, and even divers can't recognize them. They have 13 spines on their back. Normally these lie flat, but when the stonefish feels threatened, those spines pop up to deliver a deadly dose of venom.

A stonefish's venom is so strong that it may kill an adult in under an hour, unless they get a shot of **anti-venom**.

The more pressure on its spines, the more venom the stonefish will release.

An empty venom sac will be refilled in about two weeks.

26

Masters of disguise

With their skin texture and color, stonefish blend in perfectly with the reefs and rocky areas where they live. They sit perfectly still on the ocean floor, waiting for their dinner to swim by. Stonefish are patient creatures—they might stay still for hours! When small fish or crustaceans come near, the stonefish swallows them whole.

Wow!

Stonefish that are stranded on land by **low tides** can live out of the water for up to 24 hours.

Stonefish can spit water.

Stonefish can live from five to ten years in the wild.

27

Eastern screech owls

Stay still and blend in

Eastern screech owls are experts at blending in. So much so, that you could stare long and hard at a tree trunk and still not notice the little owl hiding there!

Eastern screech owls are the smallest species of owl in North America.

Hide and seek

The eastern screech owl's feathers are gray or reddish-brown with a pattern of bands and spots. This is very similar to the color and pattern of tree bark in their habitat. The camouflage is important because eastern screech owls are **nocturnal**—they rest during the day and hunt at night. They need a good disguise in the daytime so they will not become prey!

Eastern screech owls camouflage themselves in holes in tree trunks.

The owls' small size makes them very **agile**—they are even nimble enough to hunt bats.

To screech or not to screech?

Despite their name, screech owls do not screech. Instead, they make a soft **trilling** sound. Eastern screech owls mate for life and both parents help in raising their young. The smaller male usually hunts to feed his family, while the larger female protects the nest and keeps the chicks warm.

FACT FILE

Found in: Eastern North America, from Mexico to Canada

Habitat: Forests and woodlands

Height: 6.3–9.8 inches (16–25 cm)

Diet: Insects, such as beetles, moths, snails, and worms, and small mammals, such as mice and young rabbits

Wow!

Eastern screech owls have another special skill. They can fly silently because their flight feathers are **serrated** at the tips, which muffles the noise they make as they flap their wings.

Screech owls use their sharp claws to rip their food into smaller pieces.

Glossary

agile Able to move around quickly and easily

anti-venom Medication to treat bites and stings from venomous creatures

camouflage Coloring that allows an animal to hide or blend in with its surroundings

canid A member of the dog family

crustaceans Sea creatures with a hard outer shell, such as lobsters, shrimp, and crabs

cunning Clever in a secretive way

endangered When there are not many of a particular species of animal left so it is at risk of dying out

ferocious Savagely fierce or violent

hibernate To spend the winter in a resting state

ingenious Very clever and inventive

low tide When the sea is at its lowest level and farthest out from the shore

marine Describing things to do with the sea

molting When an animal sheds its skin or feathers

myth A traditional story that is not true

nocturnal Active at night

pierce To make a hole with a sharp object

predators Animals that hunt other animals for food

prey Animals that are hunted and eaten by other animals

rival Someone who competes against you

serrated Having a jagged edge

snout The long nose and mouth of an animal

trill A high-pitched warbling sound

tundra A large, treeless region in the Arctic

venomous Describing animals that are poisonous

vole A small rodent, a bit like a mouse, but with a more rounded snout

Find out more

Books

Johnson, Rebecca L. *Masters of Disguise: Amazing Animal Tricksters*. Millbrook Press, 2016.

McCormick, Anita Louise. *Devious Disguises*. Enslow Publishing, 2019.

Rabe, Tish. *High? Low? Where Did it Go?: All About Animal Camouflage*. Random House Books for Young Readers, 2016.

Websites

on.natgeo.com/2lRvLjg
Test your skills at spotting animals with National Geographic.

www.pbslearningmedia.org/resource/tdc02.sci.life.colt.disguise/masters-of-disguise/
Find out how animals use disguise to escape detection by predators or prey.

www.cbc.ca/kidscbc2/the-feed/5-animal-masters-of-disguise
Learn about five masters of disguise from the animal world.

Index